Nodejs with Koa2

NODE.JS
WITH KOA2

DEVELOP WEB APPS WITH ASYNC AND AWAIT

STEP BY STEP GUIDE
TO DEVELOP WEB APPS
WITH COMPLETE SOURCE CODE

Introduction

I assume you know JavaScript, knows web development, knows about node.js, tried it, have idea about Angularjs, Reactjs.

If you are trying to learn node.js, this book will help.

I will make your nodejs learning very easy, after reading this book, you will be able to make entire websites with nodejs using koa framework.

When I tried to learn node with koa, not much help is available online, there were absolutely not enough tutorials to help you learn, even to this date when iam writing this book, hardly any help will be there to help you build entire website from scratch, so iam writing this eBook, to help you learn faster.

Node with Koa is very easy, just like Meteorjs, if you know Meteorjs, you will know how coding is breeze, in Meteorjs, but then why not code in Meteorjs instead of node.

Although coding is breeze in Meteorjs, it is only for advance Linux user, hosting is pain, and you need to have at least intermediate levels of Linux skills to host it on VPS or dedicated server, there is no shared hosting service for meteor at the time of writing this eBook.

Meteor looked so promising and so easy, that I coded entire dating website in Meteorjs, and also hosted it, even though my hosting company gave me full support, did all the heavy lifting, still frequently website used to crash, and I was not sure what was the reason.

It does require Linux admin skills, Nginx skills and Docker skills.

If you can make websites on nodejs, they can be hosted on windows platform, websites are cool in nodejs, they are fast and real-time.

Future is micro services, software as a service; you will be developing software as a service not like in the past where you develop entire monolithic application with all the features in it, you will be building small service apps, and will be integrating other apps with it made by you or some other person.

Money is in micro service, you can develop a micro service app and upload it on cloud, and people will use your service and pay you as per use. For example you can develop an algorithm which can detect diabetes provided with some specific parameters, and people will pay you for using your algorithm, lot of services like this are available on cloud.

Why should you learn nodejs with koa

Traditional approach of software development was monolithic approach, where we have all the features in one application.

Modern approach is modular approach; this is the approach node.js uses to build software's.

Nodejs is cool, websites are fast and real-time, even though you can create websites with nodejs and express, but coding is little painful, so many call backs, it's like call back jungle, even though express framework now has generator function, but it is good to use framework which is futuristic, koa is futuristic.

Future is micro services, and they are extremely easy to code in nodejs, bulk of examples and sample code will be available of nodejs, micro services are mostly event driven, nodejs is also event driven.

Nodejs and python are the important languages to learn, lot of work is going on these two languages, you will get lot of source code for free, and you just need to know how to use it.

Iam asp.net mvc C# developer, but I learned python and nodejs, since I am also learning machine learning, lot of example code for machine learning is in python and nodejs.

I also learned math's to be able to code for machine learning and artificial intelligence, artificial intelligence will be the future, so be prepare for it.

Microsoft is lagging way behind; open source community is thriving right now.

Why it was hard to learn nodejs

We came with background with class oriented programming, from C#, Java, C, c++.

JavaScript is functional programming, and we never took JavaScript seriously, we just used it for website validation.

Why you had hard time learning nodejs, nodejs is rapidly evolving technology, framework changes happens almost every day, the code you might have got searching Google is old and absolute and no longer works, always check the date when that article was written, it was working then, but not working now, you were typing the same example code, but when you run it, it doesn't work, it is most likely that example code is absolute.

Some examples on the internet are using nodejs with Angularjs or Reactjs, that is making it more problematic to learn, you got to learn additional Angularjs framework and Reactjs framework and that confuses you, where to start what to do, it totally confuses you.

There is no need to learn Angularjs, Reactjs, for building apps with nodejs, nodejs with koa framework has everything required to make a full blown web app.

What these Angularjs, Reactjs frameworks does, they add extra layer of complexity on the app, and you waste your time to figure it out, what happened, from where this error is coming, this is where I wasted my time, when I was learning.

Angularjs, and Reactjs framework, updates and change frequently, so when you try to implement there code, it doesn't work, further increasing your frustration.

There tutorial nodejs with Angularjs are written by geeks who have no life, but to experiment and do some outstanding things in coding, and we refer these tutorials for basic learning and gets stomped.

Books available on the internet are old, outdated technology, check when it was updated, nodejs is changing very rapidly, if you buy these books with outdated techniques, it will add to your frustration.

Lot of Modules are interdependent on each other, if some modules get upgraded and you update it, it may make your code error prone, since the modules which were dependent on that module are not updated or changed completely, this is the real cause of frustration.

Each module is independently developed by geeks and they are dependent on other modules to function.

When I tried to use koa with generator function, I faced lot of problems, because some modules were abandoned by their creators and were no longer working, so I used KOA2
which has functionality like async and await much like C # code; it is implementing ECMASCRIPT 6 features.

I will also explain problems I faced and reasons behind and what I did to fix it.

Note: If you are totally new then you have to look for , what packages and package versions you are using in project, don't get confuse in packages, there are so many packages to use,

Example

For Database Connection:

monk easy, but mongoose is also good for creating schema and predefine functions For Mongodb database connection there is Monk, And mongoose:

I used monk

We are not using co-monk because co-monk doesn't work well with koa 2.0, Since co-monk uses thunkify, db.collection.find() will return a thunk, which async/await cannot handle (I think by design).

For parsing co-body and koa-bodyparser:

I found koa-bodyparser easy you have to call just app.user(bodyparser); for parsing data from pages and using ctx.request.body u will get data from forms, but in co-body you have to mention parse(this.body) for each route

For rendering koa-swig, koa-view, co-views:

I found koa-views better, just app.use(Views('foldername',{map:{html:swig}}));

And you can render pages by calling this.render('pagename');

For routing koa-route, koa-router:

Found koa-route better but it has some limitation but I didn't found those yet

For templating, too many options are available swig, handlebars, underscore and many more

Found swig better and easy for me because you don't have to do extra coding for it {%block%} is good like handlebars you can call {{datafromRoute}} and bind data in to html page{%if%}{%endif%} are easy to understand.

So choose one wisely and stick to it, after trying so many examples and tutorial finally I found some packages which are comfortable to work for me.

At starting I was too much confused between these packages and was unable to decide what to use.

For that I created separate projects for experimenting, which package is comfortable for me, and finally decided for my project, you might not agree with it you can use other packages.

This is where problem lies, which package to use and which to not, you will get some examples which use different packages to do some task, but may not work well together with alternate packages, this is where you will be wasting time, this is where you will get frustrated, that's why I have mentioned which packages I am using.

What are you going to do, about constant changes happening in nodejs and koa framework

This eBook may get absolute within 6 months, that's why I have created a website, which this book purchaser will get free access

Access code is "Married 2 Node" without double quotes.

After using this code you will be able to register on our website, where you will get free source code, and the questions about the code mentioned will be answered.

http://nodecode.info/

Some of the code may get absolute, but the latest code will be written on the website, we are developing many websites on nodejs technology, and it will be available free on the website.

In kindle edition, code written may not be seen clearly, so I will urge to visit my website and see the code.

What are you going to learn?

In this eBook, I will give you complete source code for website with basic features, login, registration, sessions, edit, and delete functions.

I will also explain how to do it and explain the code, if you get errors you can post it on our website and we will solve it.

These are the basic things for every web app, once you are able to code it, you can create any web app.

We have team of programmers who are developing next generation web apps, we will also be posting source code and discussing about it.

We are using

Node v4.4.7

Mongodb v3.2.3

Download and install node from https://nodejs.org/en/ according to your operating system

Download and install Mongodb from

https://www.mongodb.com/download-center?jmp=nav#community

Let's Start Coding

I am doing a simple project with login, registration, edit profile, delete profile and view profile. With bootstrap 3 css using bootswatch theme. We are using simple html pages and for templating swig.

Note: If you are totally new then you have to look for , what packages and package versions you are using in project, don't get confuse in packages, there are so many packages to use,

I am using Webstorm for developing web app

You can download it from here,

https://www.jetbrains.com/webstorm/download/

try trial version, and use its all features

Create new empty project in Webstorm with name loginRegitrationPract

Open terminal window at the bottom

Type following commands

npm init

This command is to create package.json file for project

Now this command will need some inserts and enters

Name: (loginRegitrationPract)loginregistrationpract // if you want to change then type the name and then press enter

Version:(1.0.0)0.0.1 // to change version type and enter

Description: koa v2 simple login registration with google project

Main:(index.js)app.js

Scripts: //note: just press enter if you don't want to fill any thing

And at last enter your package.json is ready

Now in project window you can see package.json file is created

{

  "name": " loginregistrationpract ",

```
  "version": "0.0.1",

  "description": " koa v2 simple login registration with
google project ",

  "main": "app.js",

  "scripts": {

    "test": "echo \"Error: no test specified\" && exit 1"

  },

  "keywords": [

    "koa",

    "node",

    "monk"

  ],

  "author": "Priya Patil",

  "license": "ISC"

}
```

This is how you file will look

Packages you need

- koa as a framework,
- monk for Mongodb connection
- koa-route for routing
- koa-static to parse static page
- koa-views to render views
- swig for templating
- koa-convert, koa-generic-session for sessions
- koa-bodyparser to parse page data
- passport-local, koa-passport, passport-google-auth for login and registration and authentication
- **co** for wrapping generator function because koa v2 doesn't support for it

now in terminal window type command

>npm install koa@next --save

to install latest koa version 2, '--save ' will add koa version details to package.json file under dependencies.

Open package.json and you will see

"dependencies": {
  "koa": "^2.0.0-alpha.4",

}

//note: this the current koa version but not stable you can get all the latest packages using @next after packagename but are not stable versions

And in project solution window new folder is added 'node_modules' where all project dependencies are installed

project structure will be like this

- ☐ lib
  - o db.js // to save database connection which we can access in other pages
- ☐ public
  - o css,imges,etc.. // save all css files images logos here
- ☐ routes
  - o homeRoutes.js // write down middleware module.exports function for our routes
- ☐ views   //all html pages here
  - o home.html
  - o login.html
  - o layout.html

app.js //main application file\

auth.js // authentication login registration code here

babel.app.js // to work async and await we have to use

package.json

Ok now what is this babel.app.js , for running async await functionality from koa v2 we have to run our project through babel

So we also need babel.js

Learn more about it from here

https://babeljs.io/

package.json
```
"dependencies": {
  "babel-core": "^6.13.2",
  "babel-polyfill": "^6.9.1",
  "babel-preset-es2015": "^6.13.2",
  "babel-preset-stage-0": "^6.5.0",
  "koa": "^2.0.0-alpha.4",
  "koa-bodyparser": "^3.2.0",
  "koa-convert": "^1.2.0",
  "koa-generic-session": "^1.11.3",
  "koa-passport": "^2.2.2",
  "koa-route": "^3.1.0",
  "koa-static": "^3.0.0",
  "koa-views": "^5.0.2",
  "monk": "^3.1.1",
  "passport-google-auth": "^1.0.1",
  "passport-local": "^1.0.0",
```

```
  "path": "^0.12.7",
  "swig": "^1.4.2"
}
```

You have to install all these dependencies with command

npm install <dependancyname> --save

As per our project structure create folders lib,public,routes,views

And create app.js file under your main project directory.

Got the idea, now start your project ?

A basic Hello world program to make you happy, that your code actually works, Hurray

As per our project structure create folders lib, public, routes, views and create app.js file under your main project directory.

First we will create simple app.js to run without any view or template.

./app.js
//create application object

```
var koa = require('koa');
var app = new koa();
app.use(function (ctx){
        reurn ctx.body = 'Hello World'
});
```

//this will listen your app on http://localhost:3000
```
app.listen(3000);
console.log('App listening on port 3000');
```

simple code to start your application
now in your terminal window type command

>node app

note: for koa v1 we type node --harmony app.js, but in v2 you don't have to use –harmony.

This will start your project and will show the message in terminal

App listening on port 3000

Now in a browser type localhost:3000 and you will see a hello word

Congrats, you have made your program work

Go Ahead add Some Real Code and Build your Application

Now you have been motivated, your hello world program worked, now we are going to add more functionality to our app.

Create db.js in your lib folder

./lib/db.js
```
var monk = require("monk"); //for mongodb connection
var db = monk("localhost/loginReg"); //connection to db loginReg

var db.users =db.get('users')

var users = db.users;
// we are using users collection to save users details

//this will make users available in other pages
module.exports.users = users;
```

We are using monk for database connections; we are using Mongodb in backend

We are exporting users to other modules so from any page it could be worked on.

//notes: it is compulsory to use babel or bluebird to run our project otherwise you will get error //running async await functionality

```
require("babel-core/register")({
    "presets": [
        "es2015",
        "stage-0"
    ]
});
require("babel-polyfill");
require('./app.js');
```

Now add the below code in App.js

```
var koa = require("koa");
var app = new koa();
var route = require("koa-route");
var serve = require("koa-static");
var path = require("path");
var co = require("co");

var views= require("koa-views");// to render html swig
```

template

```
app.use(views('views', {map:{html:'swig'}}));  // this will
get our html swig templates from views folder

// trust proxy
app.proxy = true;

// body parser
const bodyParser = require('koa-bodyparser');
app.use(bodyParser());

app.use(serve(__dirname + "/public"));

//routes*/
var homeRoutes = require("./routes/homeRoutes.js");
//getting js in variable

app.use(route.get("/", homeRoutes.showHome));//calling
exported function

app.listen(3000);
console.log('Listening on http://localhost:3000');
```

Now add the code in homeRoutes.js

./routes/homeRoutes.js
//async function to render home.html page

```
module.exports.showHome = async (ctx) => {

    await ctx.render('home');
}
```

Now to run this app we have to use new command window because other is running by babel

>node --harmony babel.app.js

and run

this will run our project

copy this command and paste it in package.json under scripts

```
"scripts": {
  "start": "node --harmony babel.app.js",
  "test": "echo \"Error: no test specified\" && exit 1"
}
```

Now in terminal type command

>npm start

And your project is started. Before starting our project we have to create our view pages, I am using bootswatch for bootstrap css themes

https://bootswatch.com/

./views/layout.html

```html
<!DOCTYPE html>
<html lang="en">
<head>
  <meta charset="UTF-8">
  <title>{%block title%}Title not set{%endblock%}</title>
  <link rel="stylesheet" href="/bootstrap.css">
  <link rel="stylesheet" href="/costum.css">

  <!-- HTML5 shim and Respond.js for IE8 support of HTML5 elements and media queries -->
  <!-- WARNING: Respond.js doesn't work if you view the page via file:// -->
  <!--[if lt IE 9]>
  <script src="https://oss.maxcdn.com/html5shiv/3.7.3/html5shiv.min.js"></script>
  <script src="https://oss.maxcdn.com/respond/1.4.2/respond.min.js"></script>
  <![endif]-->
</head>
<body>

<!--navbar for navigation we are already assigning links for login and logout it might give error so comment the code if error -->
```

```html
<nav class="navbar navbar-default">
  <div class="container-fluid">
    <div class="navbar-header">
      <button type="button" class="navbar-toggle collapsed" data-toggle="collapse"
              data-target="#bs-example-navbar-collapse-1">
        <span class="sr-only">Toggle navigation</span>
        <span class="icon-bar"></span>
        <span class="icon-bar"></span>
        <span class="icon-bar"></span>
      </button>
      <a class="navbar-brand" href="#">Koa test application</a>
    </div>

    <div class="collapse navbar-collapse" id="bs-example-navbar-collapse-1">
      <ul class="nav navbar-nav">
        <li><a href="/">Home </a></li>
      </ul>
<!—if you got error comment this block -->
      <ul class="nav navbar-nav navbar-right">
        {%if user === null %}
```

```html
            <li><a href="/login">Log In</a></li>
            {%else%}
            <li><a href="/members">!hi
{{user.username}}</a></li>
            <li><a href="/logout">Log Out</a></li>
            {%endif%}
         </ul>
      </div>
   </div>
</nav>
<div class="container">
   {%block content%}
   content not set
   {%endblock%}

   <footer>
      <div class="row">
         <div class="col-lg-12">
            <p>Made by <a rel="nofollow">Websol
Software Pvt. Ltd.</a>.
            </p>
         </div>
      </div>
   </footer>
</div>
```

```
</body>
</html>
```

Now Add code in home.html

// extending layout.html this will add navbar, footer and
other css used layout.html

```
{% extends 'layout.html' %}
{%block title%} Login Registration Example
{%endblock%}

{%block content%}
<div class="jumbotron">
    <h1>Welcome</h1>
    <h3>Login Registration Example</h3>
</div>
{%endblock%}
```

Now run your project, go to browser and you will see a
home page with bootstrap css

Now we will see simple login and registration with
koa-passport, passport-local and passport-google-
auth

We are going to use google authentication system for login and registration, this will prevent fake users or users with invalid email ids to register

You can create google auth key from here

https://cloud.google.com/

tutorials for creating google auth key are in plenty, you can refer them, creating google auth key is beyond the scope of this eBook, do comment or request, we may add that tutorial in our eBook, this eBook will be constantly updated and new things will be added to it.

Although Basic tutorial of google authentication is included

Create your google console project apikey and secret

for http://localhost:3000

Create ./auth.js

Add this code in your auth.js

./auth.js
```
var passport = require('koa-passport');
var db = require("./lib/db.js");
passport.serializeUser(function(user, done) {
    done(null, user._id);
```

```javascript
});
passport.deserializeUser(function(id, done) {
  db.users.findOne({_id: id}, function(err, user) {
    done(err, user);
  });
});
var LocalStrategy = require('passport-local').Strategy;
passport.use(new LocalStrategy(function(username,
password, done) {
  db.users.findOne({username:username}, function
(err,user) {
    if(err){
      done(err)
    }

    if(!user) {
      done(null, user)
    }else{
      if(username === user.username && password
=== user.password){
        done(null,user);
      }else{
        done(null, false);
      }
    }
  });
}));
```

```javascript
const GoogleStrategy = require('passport-google-
auth').Strategy;
passport.use(new GoogleStrategy({
    clientId: 'your-client-id',
    clientSecret:'your-client-secret',
    callbackURL: 'http://localhost:' +
(process.env.PORT || 3000) + '/auth/google/callback'
   },
   function (token, tokenSecret, profile, done) {

     //we are using co function to use generator function
yield functionality

     co(function *() {

       var user = yield db.users.findOne({google_id:
profile.id});
         if(!user){

         //fetch google profile and save if dose not exists
               user ={
                   name:profile.displayName,
                   email:profile.emails[0].value,
                   username:profile.emails[0].value,
                   provider:'google',
                   password:'1234',
                   google_id:profile.id,
                   imgurl:profile.image.url,
```

```
                gplusurl:profile.url,
                gender:profile.gender,
                createdAt:new Date,
                bdate:new Date,
                about:'hi there',
                updatedAt:new Date
            };
            yield db.users.insert(user);
        }

        done(null,user)
      }).catch();
    }
  ));
```

```
        module.exports = passport; // don't forget to export
```

What is this auth.js file is for?

This file is for login registration code. We are using koa-passport and passport-local for simple login and authentication.

```
        var LocalStrategy = require('passport-local').Strategy;
```

This is the local strategy where we are using passport-local. In this strategy we are getting data from login page username, password and sending result. For that first we find record for that username if found then compare with parameter username and password if true then return done(null,user); null for no errors and user to create session, and if not found or not match then return done(err,false); err for any errors found and false for no data found.

Next we are using passport-google-auth for google strategy to register by google account, So that we can make registration process fast instead of filling lengthy forms. Now in google strategy we need ouath credentials for creating google registration.

For that you have to create a project for localhost:3000 in https://console.developers.google.com and create api Key with http://localhost:3000/ and Client ID for Web application with http://localhost:3000 and http://localhost:3000/auth/google/callback and use this credentials in

```
clientId: 'your-client-id',
clientSecret:'your-client-secret',
callbackURL: 'http://localhost:' +
(process.env.PORT || 3000) +
'/auth/google/callback'
```

Now if done with this we have to write call back function for this where you have pass parameters

function (token, tokenSecret, profile, done)

Like this, in this function we are using co() wrapper to write * generator function.

To prevent duplicate registration, in this function we check if googleid already exists

var user = **yield** db.users.findOne({google_id: profile.id});

If we don't get any result then this data will be inserted in darabase and user account is created

if(!user){

```
//fetch google profile and save if dose not exists
    user ={
        name:profile.displayName,
        email:profile.emails[0].value,
        username:profile.emails[0].value,
        provider:'google',
        password:'1234',
        google_id:profile.id,
        imgurl:profile.image.url,
        gplusurl:profile.url,
        gender:profile.gender,
        createdAt:new Date,
        bdate:new Date,
        about:'hi there',
```

```
        updatedAt:new Date
    };
    yield db.users.insert(user);
}

    done(null,user)
```

And after insert we return the user with done (null,user) for creating session. Here we are retrieving user data from his google account profile like

```
    name: profile.displayName,
    email: profile.emails[0].value,
    username: profile.emails[0].value,
    provider: 'google',
    google_id: profile.id,
    imgurl: profile.image.url,
    gplusurl: profile.url,
    gender: profile.gender,
```

, name, email, googleid, gender, g+ url and image url, and also adding some additional fields to our user profile

```
    password:'1234',
    createdAt:new Date,
    bdate:new Date,
```

```
      about:'hi there',
      updatedAt:new Date
```

We are going to keep our default password '1234' for login.

Change your ./routes/homeRoutes.js like this

```
var db = require("./../lib/db.js");

var user = null;

module.exports.showHome = async (ctx) => {
   if (ctx.isAuthenticated()) {
      //console.log(ctx.passport.user);
      user = await ctx.passport.user;
   }
   await ctx.render('home', {user: user});
}
```

Now we are making some changes in homeRoutes.js

```
   if (ctx.isAuthenticated()) {
   user = await ctx.passport.user;
   }
```

here we are checking if user is already logged in then getting user data from passport session in already declared variable user

var user = **null**;
and passing this user data to home view with await render

```
await ctx.render('home', {user: user});
```

By this if there is data then it will be shown on view page else it is null. We have already written a code in our html layout page

```
{%if user === null %}
 <li><a href="/login">Log In</a></li>
{%else%}
 <li><a href="/members">!hi
{{user.username}}</a></li>
 <li><a href="/logout">Log Out</a></li>
{%endif%}
```

This means if user is logged in then it will show else links username to go to /members page and Log Out to logout. This will navigate to our members get route.

Create login.html and members.html

./views/login.html
```
{% extends 'layout.html' %}

{% block title %}Login{% endblock %}

{% block content %}
```

```html
<div class="row">
   <div class="col-lg-6 ">
      <div class="jumbotron">
         <h3>Login to your account</h3>
         <hr>
         <form action="/login" method="post" class="form-horizontal">
            <div class="form-group">
               <label for="username" class="col-lg-2 control-label">Email :</label>
               <div class="col-lg-10">
                  <input type="email" class="form-control" id="username" name="username"

placeholder="something@gmail.com">
               </div>
            </div>
            <div class="form-group">
               <label for="password" class="col-lg-2 control-label">Password:</label>
               <div class="col-lg-10">
                  <input type="password" class="form-control" id="password" name="password">
               </div>
            </div>
            <div class="form-group">
               <div class="col-lg-10 col-lg-offset-2">
                  <input type="submit" value="Log In" class="btn btn-primary">
               </div>
            </div>
```

```
        </form>
        <p>Default Password 1234 </p>
      </div>
    </div>
    <div class="col-lg-6 ">
      <p class="lead text-center">
        Or
      </p>
      <p class="text-center center-block jumbotron">
        <a href="/auth/google" class="btn btn-danger btn-
lg">Sign in with Google</a>
      </p>
    </div>
</div>
{% endblock %}
```

This is a login page with login form with post method and action '/login'

```
<form action="/login" method="post" class="form-
horizontal">
```

This means this form data will be submitted to route.post('/login' method which we are going to write in our app.js file. There are two input fields one is for username and other for password. Names of these input fields are important it should be same as we are writing in parameters of the local strategy in our auth.js file.

```html
<a href="/auth/google" class="btn btn-danger btn-lg">Sign in with Google</a>
```

There is also a link to google registration, login route, which is used to register and login both

./views/members.html

```html
{% extends 'layout.html' %}

{%block title%} Authenticated Members Area {%endblock%}

{%block content%}
<div class="jumbotron">

    <h3>Welcome {{user.username}}</h3>
<!—note: these all functionality we are going to cover in this project so for future purpose keep this links -->
    <p><a href="/edit">Edit Profile</a></p>
    <p><a href="/profile">View Profile</a></p>
    <p><a href="/delConfirm">Delete Me</a></p>
</div>

{%endblock%}
```

This is our members.html file which we are going to user to redirect after login is successful. Here we are taking username name of logged in user

{{user.username}}

Like this, this user we will get from passport.user. Remaining links are of no use because we have not created route or pages for that, but keep them as we develop our project this is going to be in use. If getting error then comment it for the time being.

Now in ./app.js we have to add some routes and declarations for login registration.

```
./app.js
var koa = require("koa");
var app = new koa();

var route = require("koa-route");
var serve = require("koa-static");
var path = require("path");
var co = require("co");
var views= require("koa-views");

app.use(views('views', {map:{html:'swig'}}));

// trust proxy
app.proxy = true;


// sessions
const convert = require('koa-convert');
const session = require('koa-generic-session');
app.keys = ['your-session-secret', 'another-session-
```

```
secret'];
app.use(convert(session()));


// body parser
const bodyParser = require('koa-bodyparser');
app.use(bodyParser());

app.use(serve(__dirname + "/public"));

// authentication
require('./auth');
var passport = require('koa-passport');
app.use(passport.initialize());
app.use(passport.session());

//routes*/
var homeRoutes = require("./routes/homeRoutes.js");
var loginRoutes = require("./routes/loginRoutes.js");
var membersRoutes =
require("./routes/membersRoutes.js");

app.use(route.get("/", homeRoutes.showHome));
app.use(route.get('/login',loginRoutes.showLogin));
app.use(route.get('/logout',loginRoutes.logout));

app.use(route.get('/members',membersRoutes.showMe
m));

// POST /login
app.use(route.post('/login',
```

```
    passport.authenticate('local', {
       successRedirect: '/members',
       failureRedirect: '/login?err=local'
    })
));


app.use(route.get('/auth/google',
    passport.authenticate('google',{session:false,
scope:['email','profile'], accessType: 'offline',
approvalPrompt: 'force'}
    )));

app.use(route.get('/auth/google/callback',
    passport.authenticate('google', {
       successRedirect: '/members',
       failureRedirect: '/login?err=google'
    })
));

app.listen(3000);
console.log('Listening on http://localhost:3000');
```

In the below code we are adding session functionalities
to our webapp

```
    // sessions
    const convert = require('koa-convert');
    const session = require('koa-generic-session');
    app.keys = ['your-session-secret', 'another-session-
```

```
    secret'];
    app.use(convert(session()));
```

Koa-generic-session for creating session at login and registration, Koa-convert is for wrapper around the session and app.keys for storing this as cookie in browser encoded secretly.

```
    require('./auth');
```

With this above line we are getting all data written in auth.js file. Next we are initializing and creating session by passing passport to app like this

```
    app.use(passport.initialize());
    app.use(passport.session());
```

 next we are going to create routes for login to get and post data. And members and logout routes also

```
app.use(route.get('/login',loginRoutes.showLogin));
app.use(route.get('/logout',loginRoutes.logout));
app.use(route.get('/members',membersRoutes.showMe
m));
```

This is the get method for /login route which is calling other method showLogin from our middleware which we are going write next. Also logout from loginRoutes and showMem from membersRoutes.

```
// POST /login
app.use(route.post('/login',
    passport.authenticate('local', {
        successRedirect: '/members',
        failureRedirect: '/login?err=local'
    })
));
```

This is the post method which going to get all form data and passing it to our local strategy in auth.js file which I have already explained. And if the result come out as true then it will create session for user and redirect to '/members' route, and if result is false then it will redirect to login page with error.

```
app.use(route.get('/auth/google',
    passport.authenticate('google',{session:false,
scope:['email','profile'], accessType: 'offline',
approvalPrompt: 'force'}
    )));
```

Next route is for google registration /auth/google this will send request to google for profile and email details of already logged in google user, and forward it to our auth.js google strategy function, and then it sends the result to our callback route.

```
app.use(route.get('/auth/google/callback',
        passport.authenticate('google', {
```

```
          successRedirect: '/members',
          failureRedirect: '/login?err=google'
          })
    ));
```

Here the callback route will verifies the result if true then creates session and redirect to '/members' and else redirects to login with error, because our '/auth/google' link is on same page. User can either use login form or google signup button to login, because we are checking if googleid already exist then it forwards the user data to create login session in our auth.js file.

Now next we will write our middleware functions for '/login' route, and '/members' route /logout

Write the code in

./routes/loginRoutes.js

```
var db = require("./../lib/db.js");

// to show our login page
module.exports.showLogin = async(ctx) => {
    await  ctx.render("login");
};

//to log out
module.exports.logout = async(ctx) => {
```

```
    ctx.logout();
    ctx.session = null;
    ctx.redirect('/');
};
```

We are getting db object from our db.js file from lib directory where we have created connection with database and users collection.

```
module.exports.showLogin = async(ctx) => {
```

This line will export our showLogin async function which is accessible in our app.js file by creating variable with require keyword.

```
await ctx.render("login");
```

This will render our html page in asynchronies manner because we are using await key word. Next is our logout function by which we logout the user from auth and empty the session and redirect it to home page.

Now write the code in

./routes/membersRoutes.js

```
var db = require("./../lib/db.js");

var user = null;

module.exports.showMem = async (ctx) => {
    //to check if user is logged in
```

```
    if (ctx.isAuthenticated()) {
        user = await ctx.passport.user;
    } else {
        ctx.redirect("/");
    }
    await ctx.render("members", { user:
JSON.stringify(user, null, 2)});
};
```

this is membersRoute module where we are creating
showMem function, where first we verify if user is
authenticated if user is logged in then it will get the user
data in user variable which we have already declared
null and then rendered members page with user.

await ctx.render("members", { user: JSON.stringify(user,
null, 2)});

before running your project don't forget to run Mongodb,
run project, from menu bar navigate to login page
register with google auth button, you will be asked to
login to your google account after login you will get the
page where you have to allow access to your email and
profile details, and then you will be redirected to
members page with your email on page. If you don't see
anything or got error not found, internal server error..etc .
go to your terminal you will get error details there, if don't
then try to use console.log(); in your code and this will

show what data you are getting. If registered successfully then check mongodb for database loginReg and collection users check if data is inserted, I am using robomongo for mongodb where I can check users collection easily. Try to logout and login using username, password in login form, by default we are using password:'1234' so try to login with it and logout again.

Now next we will learn to update profile, view profile and delete profile functionality

For that we have to create new routes for get and post for edit, get profile and delete

Create ./routes/editRoutes.js

./routes/editRoutes.js
```
var db = require("./../lib/db.js");

module.exports.editUser = async (ctx) =>{
   if(ctx.isAuthenticated()){
        try {
           var user =  ctx.passport.user;

            await ctx.render("edit",user);
        }catch(ex){
            console.log(ex)
        }
```

```javascript
    }else{
        ctx.redirect('/');
    }
};

//post method to update data
module.exports.updateUser = async(ctx)=>{
    if(ctx.isAuthenticated()){
        var id = ctx.passport.user._id;
        var postedData =ctx.request.body;

        // console.log(postedData);
        var userToUpdate = {
            name : postedData.name,
            gender:postedData.gender,
            bdate:postedData.bdate,
            password:postedData.password,
            about:postedData.about,
            updatedAt:new Date
        }
        //console.log(userToUpdate);
        await
db.users.update({_id:id},{$set:userToUpdate});

        ctx.redirect('profile');

    }else{
        ctx.redirect('/');
    }
};
module.exports.delConfirm = async(ctx)=>{
```

```
    await ctx.render('delConfirm');
}

//to delete your profile from database
module.exports.delUser = async(ctx)=>{
    if(ctx.isAuthenticated()){
        var id = await ctx.passport.user._id;

        db.users.remove({_id:id});
//this will clear sessions and redirect to login page
        ctx.logout();
        ctx.session = null;
        ctx.redirect('/login');

    }else{
        ctx.render('/');
    }
}
```

This is our editRoute.js where first we are getting our db in db variable then we create our get edit page function, where we first verify user with isAuthenticated() if user is loggd in then we get his data from session and pass it to our page by render

await ctx.render("edit",user);

Like this we can access logged in user data into our edit form which we will create in edit.html page. Next function is for post route of edit form where we get all posted data bay form in to our middleware, with the help of koa-bodyparser which we have already declared and used in our app of app.js file.

var postedData =ctx.request.body;

This is how we get the data from form to the postedData variable, only logged in user is allowed to update profile, so we are checking isAuthenticated then getting userid in to id variable from our session

var id = ctx.passport.user._id;
using this line of code. Now when we got id and data both we move next to update the data in database

```
var userToUpdate = {
    name : postedData.name,
    gender:postedData.gender,
    bdate:postedData.bdate,
    password:postedData.password,
    about:postedData.about,
    updatedAt:new Date
}
```

In userToUpdate variable we writing the data in which we are going to write in mongo update query. In short we are giving functionality to users to update their profile

await db.users.update({_id:id},{$set:userToUpdate});

By this command we are matching existing user id with the database and updating data with the $set key word by this only that field will be updated which are mentioned in the query and remaining fields will be same. After that redirected to the profile where user can see updated data and full profile.

Now ./routes/profileRoutes.js

```
./routes/profileRoutes.js
var db = require("./../lib/db.js");

module.exports.showProfile = async (ctx) =>{
    if(ctx.isAuthenticated()){

        try {
            var user =  ctx.passport.user;

            //console.log(vm);
            await ctx.render("profile",user);

        }catch(ex){
            console.log(ex)
        }
    }else{
        ctx.redirect('/');
    }
};
```

This is membersRoutes.js page where again we writing a get route function of profile page. Similar to edit page we verifying user getting data from session passing it to members.html page with render

await ctx.render("profile",user);

And if not authenticated then redirected to home

Now it's time to add some more code to our ./app.js file

Last changes in this file

./app.js

```
var koa = require("koa");
var app = new koa();

var route = require("koa-route");
var serve = require("koa-static");
var path = require("path");
var co = require("co");
var views= require("koa-views");

app.use(views('views', {map:{html:'swig'}}));

// trust proxy
app.proxy = true;

// sessions
const convert = require('koa-convert');
```

```
const session = require('koa-generic-session');
app.keys = ['your-session-secret', 'another-session-
secret'];
app.use(convert(session()));

// body parser
const bodyParser = require('koa-bodyparser');
app.use(bodyParser());

app.use(serve(__dirname + "/public"));

// authentication
require('./auth');
var passport = require('koa-passport');
app.use(passport.initialize());
app.use(passport.session());

//routes*/
var homeRoutes = require("./routes/homeRoutes.js");
var loginRoutes = require("./routes/loginRoutes.js");
var membersRoutes =
require("./routes/membersRoutes.js");
var editRoutes = require("./routes/editRoutes.js");
var profileRoutes = require("./routes/profileRoutes.js");

app.use(route.get("/", homeRoutes.showHome));

app.use(route.get('/login',loginRoutes.showLogin));
app.use(route.get('/logout',loginRoutes.logout));

app.use(route.get('/members',membersRoutes.showMe
```

```
m));
app.use(route.get('/profile',profileRoutes.showProfile));

app.use(route.get('/edit',editRoutes.editUser));
app.use(route.post('/edit',editRoutes.updateUser));
app.use(route.get('/delConfirm',editRoutes.delConfirm));
app.use(route.get('/deluser',editRoutes.delUser));

// POST /login
app.use(route.post('/login',
    passport.authenticate('local', {
        successRedirect: '/members',
        failureRedirect: '/login?err=local'
    })
));

app.use(route.get('/auth/google',
    passport.authenticate('google',{session:false,
scope:['email','profile'], accessType: 'offline',
approvalPrompt: 'force'}
    )));

app.use(route.get('/auth/google/callback',
    passport.authenticate('google', {
        successRedirect: '/members',
        failureRedirect: '/login?err=google'
    })
));

app.listen(3000);
console.log('Listening on http://localhost:3000');
```

This is probably our last changes in app.js file, adding some routes for edit, profile.

```
var editRoutes = require("./routes/editRoutes.js");
var profileRoutes = require("./routes/profileRoutes.js");
```

Creating variables for editRoutes and profileRutes.

To show profile page get method is called
app.use(route.get('/profile',profileRoutes.showProfile));

For edit get and post routes are created
app.use(route.get('/edit',editRoutes.editUser));
app.use(route.post('/edit',editRoutes.updateUser));

And for delete we are calling two routes first page to confirm the deletion and second one is to delete user

app.use(route.get('/delConfirm',editRoutes.delConfirm));
app.use(route.get('/deluser',editRoutes.delUser));

and now finally create html pages for edit form , profile view and delete confirmation.

./views/edit.html

```
{% extends 'layout.html' %}

{% block title %} New Question {% endblock %}

{% block content %}
<div class="row">
   <div class="col-lg-6 col-lg-offset-3">
      <div class="jumbotron">
         <h3>Update your Account</h3>
         <hr>
         <form class="form-horizontal" name="editForm"
action="/edit" method="post" role="form">
            <div class="form-group">
               <label for="username" class="col-lg-2
control-label">Email :</label>
               <div class="col-lg-10">
                  {{username}}
                  <!--<input type="email" class="form-
control" id="email" name="email"
                     value="{{email}}">-->
               </div>
            </div>
            <div class="form-group">
               <label for="name" class="col-lg-2 control-
label">Name :</label>
               <div class="col-lg-10">

                  <input type="text" class="form-control"
id="name" name="name"
                     value="{{name}}">
```

```html
                </div>
            </div>
            <div class="form-group">
                <label for="password" class="col-lg-2
control-label">Password:</label>
                <div class="col-lg-10">
                    <input type="text" class="form-control"
id="password" name="password" value="{{password}}">
                </div>
            </div>
            <div class="form-group">
                <label class="col-lg-2 control-
label">Gender</label>
                <div class="col-lg-10">
                    <div class="radio">
                        <label>
                            <input type="radio" name="gender"
id="genderM" value="male" {%if gender ===
'male'%}checked=""{%endif%}>
                            <label for="genderM">Male</label>
                        </label>
                    </div>
                    <div class="radio">
                        <label>
                            <input type="radio" name="gender"
id="genderF" value="female" {%if gender ===
'female'%}checked=""{%endif%}>
                            <label
for="genderF">Female</label>
                        </label>
                    </div>
```

```
                </div>
            </div>
            <div class="form-group">
                <label for="bdate" class="col-lg-2 control-
label">Birth Date:</label>
                <div class="col-lg-10">
                    <input type="date" class="form-control"
id="bdate" name="bdate" value="{{bdate}}">
                </div>
            </div>
            <div class="form-group">
                <label for="about" class="col-lg-2 control-
label">About you:</label>
                <div class="col-lg-10">
                    <textarea type="text" class="form-control"
id="about" name="about" >{{about}}</textarea>
                </div>
            </div>
            <div class="form-group">
                <div class="col-lg-10 col-lg-offset-2">
                    <input type="submit" value="Update"
class="btn btn-primary">
                </div>
            </div>
        </form>
    </div>
  </div>
</div>
{% endblock %}
```

This forms three new fields to our user data which we have inserted while registration with some default date birthdate, about and updatedDate which we add by new date(). And also password, name can be modified by user. This form has 'post' method to '/edit' action.

Functionality for viewprofile, add code

./views/profile.html
```
{% extends 'layout.html'%}

{% block title %} {{name}}'s profile{%endblock%}

{%block content%}
<div class="row">
   <div class="col-lg-4">
      <img src="{{imgurl.replace("?sz=50","")}}"
class="img-responsive">
   </div>
   <div class="col-lg-8">
      <h1>{{name}}</h1>
      <p>Birth date :{{bdate.toString()}}</p>
      <p>Gender : {{gender}}</p>
      <p>Join date : {{createdAt.toString()}}</p>
      <p>About me : {{about}}</p>
   </div>
</div>

{%endblock%}
```

Confirm users before deleting, add this code to confirm delete

./views/delConfirm.html

```
{% extends 'layout.html' %}

{%block title%}delete confirmation{%endblock%}

{%block content%}
<div class="jumbotron">
    <p><a href="/deluser">Are you shore? You want
to delete this profile??? </a></p>
</div>
{%endblock%}
```

Try run project login edit profile check database for changes delete profile this links we have already given in members.html page navigate from there. Again found error try to solve it by reading terminal window using console.log and you will find easy to solve it

This is the basic functionality we have gave you to start your journey to start developing application in node, once you are used to basic functionality you can later on develop complex applications

How to host project on Windows Sever 2008 R2

Requirement:

- Dedicated server Windows 2008 R2
- ISS 7.5
- Node
- IISNode
- URL rewrite module for IIS

You should have good knowledge of iis manager, configuration of websites and security permissions.

Node:

- Download and install latest stable version from
- https://nodejs.org/en/
- This will install node to c:/program files/nodejs

IISNode

- Download and install IISNode from https://github.com/azure/iisnode/wiki/iisnode-releases according to os 32 or 64, I downloaded iisnode for iis 7/8 (x64) because my os is 64 bit

- This will download in c:/program files/iisnode, go to iis manager and click on any sites and check modules you can see iisnode is added to it

URL rewrite module for IIS

- Download and install from http://www.iis.net/downloads/microsoft/url-rewrite

Configure application for hosting

Now we have to do some changes to our application, like adding web.confige file, setting app.listen port and some changes in auth code.

Ok now hosting my site on http://websolnetwork.com/ with the help of Remote Desktop connection I am accessing my server.

Before uploading site add web.config file in app root folder.

./web.config

```
<configuration>
    <appSettings>
        <add key="BABEL_DISABLE_CACHE"
value="true" />
    </appSettings>
    <system.webServer>
```

```xml
        <!-- indicates that the hello.js file is a node.js
application
    to be handled by the iisnode module -->

        <handlers>
            <add name="iisnode"
path="babel.app.js" verb="*" modules="iisnode" />
        </handlers>
        <rewrite>
            <rules>
                <rule name="NodeInspector"
patternSyntax="ECMAScript" stopProcessing="true">
                    <match
url="^babel.app.js\/debug[\/]?" />
                </rule>
                <rule name="LoginReg">
                    <match url="/*" />
                    <action type="Rewrite"
url="babel.app.js" />
                </rule>
            </rules>
        </rewrite>
        <!--
    the iisnode section configures the behavior of the
node.js IIS module
    setting values below are defaults

    * node_env - determines the environment (production,
development, staging, ...) in which
    child node processes run; if nonempty, is propagated
to the child node processes as their NODE_ENV
```

environment variable; the default is the value of the IIS worker process'es NODE_ENV environment variable

* nodeProcessCommandLine - command line starting the node executable; in shared hosting environments this setting would typically be locked at the machine scope.

* interceptor - fully qualified file name of a node.js application that will run instead of an actual application the request targets; the fully qualified file name of the actual application file is provided as the first parameter to the interceptor application; default interceptor supports iisnode logging

* nodeProcessCountPerApplication - number of node.exe processes that IIS will start per application; setting this value to 0 results in creating one node.exe process per each processor on the machine

* maxConcurrentRequestsPerProcess - maximum number of reqeusts one node process can handle at a time

* maxNamedPipeConnectionRetry - number of times IIS will retry to establish a named pipe connection with a node process in order to send a new HTTP request

* namedPipeConnectionRetryDelay - delay in milliseconds between connection retries

* maxNamedPipeConnectionPoolSize - maximum number of named pipe connections that will be kept in a connection pool;
    connection pooling helps improve the performance of applications that process a large number of short lived HTTP requests

* maxNamedPipePooledConnectionAge - age of a pooled connection in milliseconds after which the connection is not reused for
    subsequent requests

* asyncCompletionThreadCount - size of the IO thread pool maintained by the IIS module to process asynchronous IO; setting it
    to 0 (default) results in creating one thread per each processor on the machine

* initialRequestBufferSize - initial size in bytes of a memory buffer allocated for a new HTTP request

* maxRequestBufferSize - maximum size in bytes of a memory buffer allocated per request; this is a hard limit of
    the serialized form of HTTP request or response headers block

* watchedFiles - semi-colon separated list of files that will be watched for changes; a change to a file causes the application to recycle;

each entry consists of an optional directory name plus required file name which are relative to the directory where the main application entry point
is located; wild cards are allowed in the file name portion only; for example:
"*.js;node_modules\foo\lib\options.json;app_data*.config.json"

* uncFileChangesPollingInterval - applications are recycled when the underlying *.js file is modified; if the file resides
on a UNC share, the only reliable way to detect such modifications is to periodically poll for them; this setting
controls the polling interval

* gracefulShutdownTimeout - when a node.js file is modified, all node processes handling running this application are recycled;
this setting controls the time (in milliseconds) given for currently active requests to gracefully finish before the
process is terminated; during this time, all new requests are already dispatched to a new node process based on the fresh version
of the application

* loggingEnabled - controls whether stdout and stderr streams from node processes are captured and made available over HTTP

* logDirectory - directory name relative to the main application file that will store files with stdout and stderr captures;
individual log file names have unique file names; log files are created lazily (i.e. when the process actually writes something
to stdout or stderr); an HTML index of all log files is also maintained as index.html in that directory;
by default, if your application is at http://foo.com/bar.js, logs will be accessible at http://foo.com/iisnode;
SECURITY NOTE: if log files contain sensitive information, this setting should be modified to contain enough entropy to be considered
cryptographically secure; in most situations, a GUID is sufficient

* debuggingEnabled - controls whether the built-in debugger is available

* debuggerPortRange - range of TCP ports that can be used for communication between the node-inspector debugger and the debugee; iisnode
will round robin through this port range for subsequent debugging sessions and pick the next available (free) port to use from the range

* debuggerPathSegment - URL path segment used to access the built-in node-inspector debugger; given a node.js application at

http://foo.com/bar/baz.js, the debugger can be accessed at http://foo.com/bar/baz.js/{debuggerPathSegment}, by default
http://foo.com/bar/baz.js/debug

* debugHeaderEnabled - boolean indicating whether iisnode should attach the iisnode-debug HTTP response header with
diagnostics information to all responses

* maxLogFileSizeInKB - maximum size of a single log file in KB; once a log file exceeds this limit a new log file is created

* maxTotalLogFileSizeInKB - maximum total size of all log files in the logDirectory; once exceeded, old log files are removed

* maxLogFiles - maximum number of log files in the logDirectory; once exceeded, old log files are removed

* devErrorsEnabled - controls how much information is sent back in the HTTP response to the browser when an error occurrs in iisnode;
when true, error conditions in iisnode result in HTTP 200 response with the body containing error details; when false,
iisnode will return generic HTTP 5xx responses

* flushResponse - controls whether each HTTP response body chunk is immediately flushed by iisnode; flushing each body chunk incurs
    CPU cost but may improve latency in streaming scenarios

* enableXFF - controls whether iisnode adds or modifies the X-Forwarded-For request HTTP header with the IP address of the remote host

* promoteServerVars - comma delimited list of IIS server variables that will be propagated to the node.exe process in the form of
    x-iisnode-<server_variable_name> HTTP request headers; for a list of IIS server variables available see
    http://msdn.microsoft.com/en-us/library/ms524602(v=vs.90).aspx; for example "AUTH_USER,AUTH_TYPE"

* configOverrides - optional file name containing overrides of configuration settings of the iisnode section of web.config;
    the format of the file is a small subset of YAML: each setting is represented as a <key>: <value> on a separate line
    and comments start with # until the end of the line, e.g.
        # This is a sample iisnode.yml file
        nodeProcessCountPerApplication: 2
        maxRequestBufferSize: 8192 # increasing from the default

```
        # maxConcurrentRequestsPerProcess: 512 -
commented out setting



        <iisnode
        node_env="%node_env%"
        nodeProcessCountPerApplication="1"

maxConcurrentRequestsPerProcess="1024"
        maxNamedPipeConnectionRetry="100"
        namedPipeConnectionRetryDelay="250"
        maxNamedPipeConnectionPoolSize="512"

maxNamedPipePooledConnectionAge="30000"
        asyncCompletionThreadCount="0"
        initialRequestBufferSize="4096"
        maxRequestBufferSize="65536"
        watchedFiles="*.js;iisnode.yml"
        uncFileChangesPollingInterval="5000"
        gracefulShutdownTimeout="60000"
        loggingEnabled="true"
        logDirectory="iisnode"
        debuggingEnabled="true"
        debugHeaderEnabled="false"
        debuggerPortRange="5058-6058"
        debuggerPathSegment="debug"
        maxLogFileSizeInKB="128"
        maxTotalLogFileSizeInKB="1024"
        maxLogFiles="20"
        devErrorsEnabled="true"
```

```
            flushResponse="false"
            enableXFF="false"
            promoteServerVars=""
            configOverrides="iisnode.yml"
    />
-->
            <!--


    One more setting that can be modified is the path to
the node.exe executable and the interceptor:
    <iisnode
nodeProcessCommandLine="&quot;%programfiles%\no
dejs\node.exe&quot;" /> -->
    <iisnode

nodeProcessCommandLine="&quot;%programfiles%\no
dejs\node.exe&quot;"

interceptor="&quot;%programfiles%\iisnode\interceptor.js
&quot;"
        loggingEnabled="true"
            logDirectory="iisnode"
        debuggerExtensionDll="iisnode-inspector.dll"
            debuggingEnabled="true"
            debugHeaderEnabled="false"
            debuggerPortRange="5058-6058"
            debuggerPathSegment="debug"
            maxLogFileSizeInKB="128"
            maxTotalLogFileSizeInKB="1024"
            maxLogFiles="20"
        />
```

```
        </system.webServer>
</configuration>
```

Ok now some explanation of we are doing in web.confige file

```
<handlers>
        <add name="iisnode" path="babel.app.js" verb="*"
modules="iisnode" />
</handlers>
```

This where we show the path="babel.app.js" this our main application file to start application, remember we are running our app with babel.

```
<rewrite>
        <rules>
                <rule name="NodeInspector"
patternSyntax="ECMAScript" stopProcessing="true">
                <match url="^babel.app.js\/debug[\/]?" />
                </rule>
                <rule name="LoginReg">
                        <match url="/*" />
                        <action type="Rewrite"
url="babel.app.js" />
                </rule>
```

```
    </rules>
</rewrite>
```

This is our url rewrite code for that you have to install URL rewrite module for IIS on your server first, by this code when you type http://websitname.com then it will automatically call babel.app.js file. If this code is note in your config file then you have to type http://websitname.com/babel.app.js and then it will run your app.

```
<iisnode
nodeProcessCommandLine="&quot;%programfiles%\no
dejs\node.exe&quot;" /> -->
    <iisnode

nodeProcessCommandLine="&quot;%programfiles%\no
dejs\node.exe&quot;"

interceptor="&quot;%programfiles%\iisnode\interceptor.js
&quot;"
        loggingEnabled="true"
        logDirectory="iisnode"
        debuggerExtensionDll="iisnode-inspector.dll"
        debuggingEnabled="true"
        debugHeaderEnabled="false"
        debuggerPortRange="5058-6058"
        debuggerPathSegment="debug"
        maxLogFileSizeInKB="128"
        maxTotalLogFileSizeInKB="1024"
```

maxLogFiles="20"
/>

Ok with this line of code we are showing our node.exe file path and issnode file path to our application. Logging enabled true this will create a iisnode directory in application folder and save log files in it. You can access it by websitname.com/iisnode/index.html.

Ok now before uploading we have to remove node_modules folder from application folder, or else it will take forever to upload. Don't delete it directly delete it from command-prompt

Open command-prompt goto application directory and type following command

>rmdir node_modules/s

/? Will show you options for delete

After this some changes in app.js file

./app.js
```
//this will listen your app on http://localhost:3000
app.listen(3000);
console.log('App listening on port 3000');
```

Remember previously we have wrote this code in our app.js file now change it to this

```
var port = process.env.PORT || 3000;

app.listen(port);

console.log("App is listening on port " + port);
```

process.env.PORT this will get the running port which port 80 or else we are running it locally then it will take port 3000.

Ok remember console Google API console we have created for localhost:3000 now create it for your website. Change it in ./auth.js file. Also change callback url to http://websitname.com/auth/google/callback.

Ok now upload your app on your server using ftp.
- Now on server create a separate folder in c:/ with name test copy paste your app in it.
- Go to command prompt with administrator permission go to your c:/test/application directory and type
- >npm install
- This will install all the dependencies in your application directory under node_modules folder.
- Now go to your IIS Manager.
- At left pane there is list of sites under site folder, if you have already created web site then you will

find your site there, else create it, right click on site folder add website.

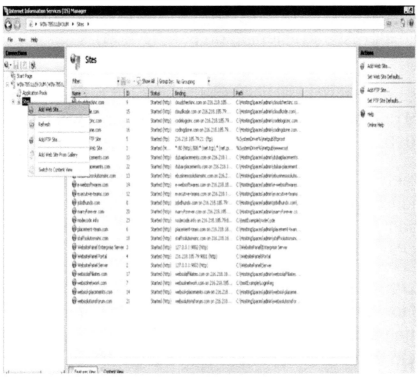

- My site is already created using website panel.
- Now click on site name go to basic settings,

- change application pool to DefaultAppPool,

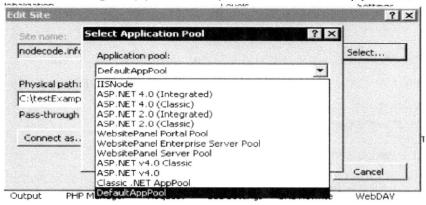

- change physical path to you application
c:/test/applicationDirectory

- click test settings this will show warning cannot verify access to path c:/test/applicationdirectory but neglect it it's just a warning

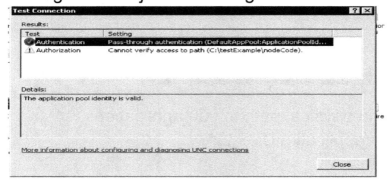

- Ok now close click ok
- Right click on site name click edit permission go to security, see under groups or user names: there is a list of users see if there is a DefaultAppPool,

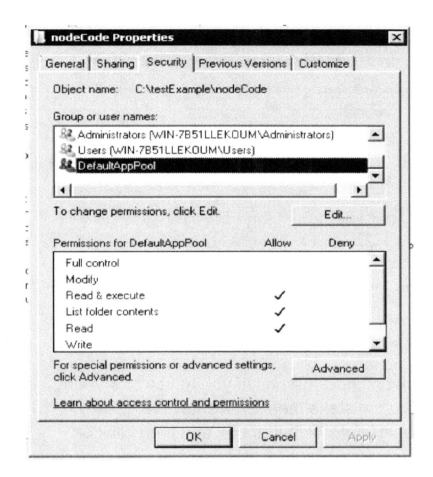

- if not then click edit then add, under enter object name to select, type
- IIS AppPool\DefaultAppPool

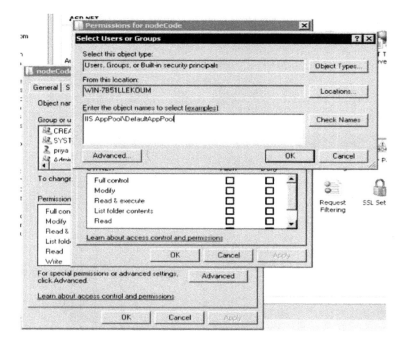

- Click on check names, if you haven't done any speling mistake then it will show the DefaultAppPool in that box and then click ok

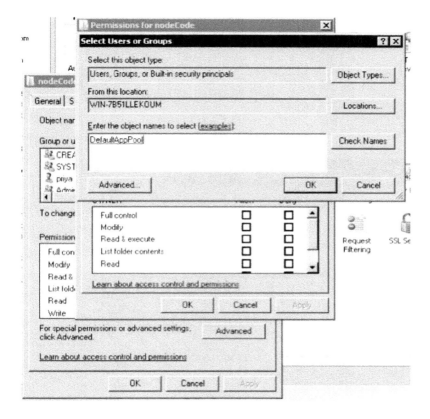

- Now click apply, it will take some time to assign permission to your node_modules folder.
- After it click ok may be two times.
- Now you have to assign some permission to iisnode, node.exe in c:/programfile to access by IIS_USRS

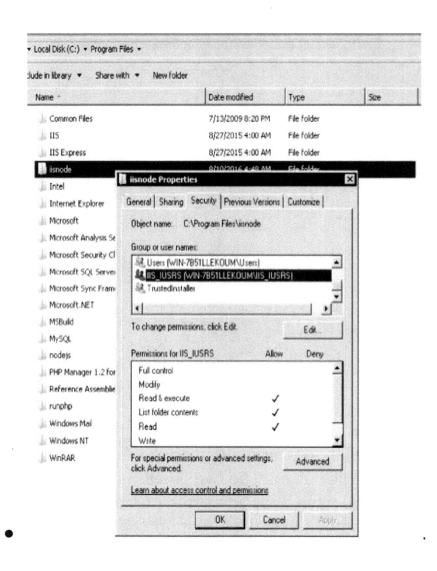

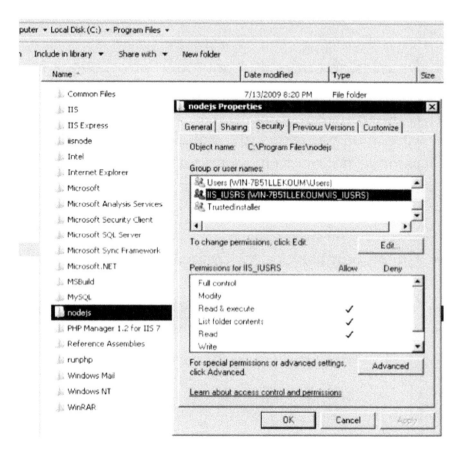

- Same procedure right click security, check for IIS_USRS else, edit, add user type IIS_USRS check names and click ok
- Remember no spelling mistakes.
- Ok done now got to browser and type your sitename

Errors I got when hosting and how I fixed it

- Permission errors 404 not found error, check for permissions you have assign to node.exe and iisnode-inspector.dll
- Check all packages are installed properly else remove node_modules and again install all packages using administrator command prompt, after doing this again assign permissions to your site from iis manager
- Check permissions for DefaultAppPool read/write execute are assigned
- You may found error IISNode configuration error
- Go to appsite iismanager right click recycle apppool

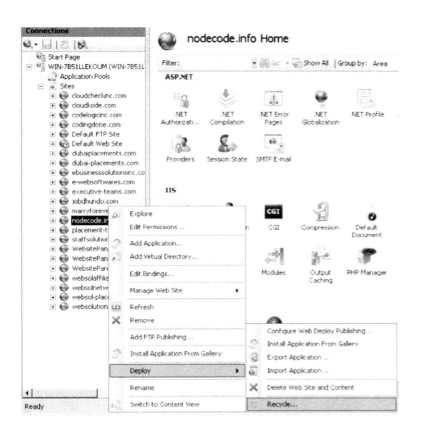

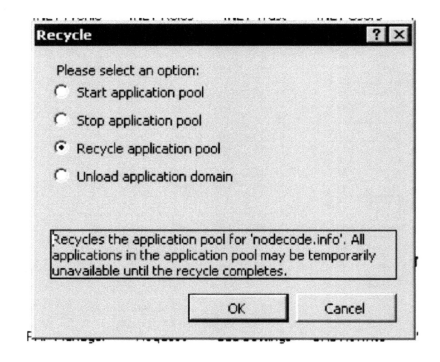

- After this or after creating changes in app files it will show error for some time, because it recycles the apppool after changes so don't worry it will be resolved after some time.
- This will solve your error

Errors You May Face

While create this project I came across many errors, because there are no proper examples available on the internet, hours are spent fixing the bug, you may get small patches like how to use passport for login registration but that example may be not using same packages like us, so it will be hard to understand and modify according to your packages, again you have to search for v2 coding where you are using async await but there are very few examples available, you will get v1 examples more for koa.

While using async await you should be careful, don't use too many await it will throw error, you should know where to use await and where not. While routing don't redirect too much it will throw to-many-redirects error on browser and you have to clear your browser cache, remove redirects and then run the project.

If you are used to generator functions then try to use co.

You can go for testing using mocha, supertest, you should simultaneously run test project you will find easy to understand your project. Use try catch for handling errors, in db queries use function(err,data) in callback so you will know you are getting data or not. Be proper with declarations, names and be sure all packages are installed. Check for terminal every time you run your project and while rendering pages on browser.

Downloading the Entire Project and using it

You can download the entire project from here
http://www.aminnagpure.com/p/nodejs-with-koa2-source-code.html

And after that from command prompt, get to that folder and

Type "npm install" without quotes

That will install all the packages mentioned in package.json, and your application is ready to go

Best of luck in your journey as a node programmer

You can modify the program and add features the way you want

If you have any problems with the code, you can comment on that web page

About Us

Amin B Nagpure

Programmer, Web Developer

You can follow me on
http://www.aminnagpure.com